Secrets of Mount Kailash, Bermuda Triangle and the Lost City of Atlantis

By

Jagdish Krishanlal Arora

techbagg@outlook.com

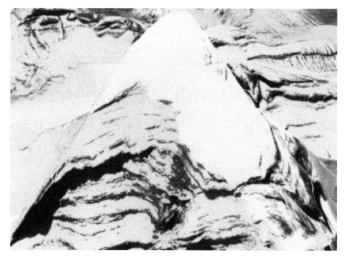

IMAGE: MOUNT KAILASH (Source: Google Earth)

Introduction

I have written books on several different subjects and before writing them watched several hundreds of videos, read several thousands of texts on the internet and read several hundreds of books. It takes a lot of efforts to write a book and it is tough completing even a single book. When I write the hand just moves and keeps on typing and typing and if I stop the book remains incomplete so in order to complete the book. I have to finish it as quickly as I can before the mood changes and I become lazy. If I write everything I know about the Earth, space, planets, galaxy and the universe it would fill a thousand books or more.

But the spinal cord in my body pains when I start writing, and sometimes it is tough on the mind because I am sharing great knowledge. The reason is going through a lot of information and verification of its authenticity puts a huge load on the mind and it also gets overloaded like computers. The things I write you will have to read several articles, watch several videos and read several books to gain which I give you only in a few books of mine. Most of the things I write automatically using stored information in my mind and then some necessary information which required statistics and verification I have to check several sources before writing it down.

When I first started reading spirituality and mysticism it took me lot of days to understand a simple paragraph, but as I read regularly, I was able to understand things more clearly. The same is applicable here, when you read my books, if they are not clear the first time, you need to read them again and again or a

Image: Mount Kailash (Source: Google Earth)

few pages at a time. Then only you will be clear about what you read and understand. The mind behaves very erratically and it takes time for the mind to gain and store whatever it sees, feels and reads and understand practical things we do every day.

Something which I am unable to understand many things. I then go through them several times, till my mind is clear about them. Nobody is perfect not even God. You also have to go through some of the things several times till you understand them if it is not clear at the first reading.

To make the book interesting I have included several images/illustrations under the common license and general attribution license to give you an overall picture of what it is to be like to be there in actual.

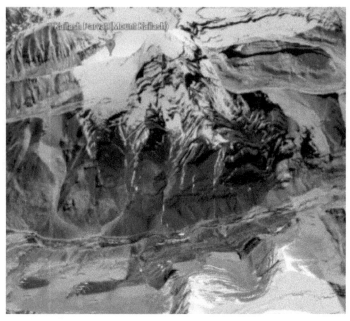

Image: Mount Kailash. The red pointer is the mark where it is the highest point you can go. Beyond that it becomes difficult. (Source: Google Earth)

The Beginning

M ount Kailash lies in the Tibet Autonomous Region of China and is 6700 meters high (22,000 ft). Bermuda triangle is also known as the Devil's triangle and is a region located in the western part of the North Atlantic Ocean near to Florida. In the Bermuda triangle it is said that ships and planes disappear when travelling over the area. The exact area where the ships disappear is not clearly identified and extends over to a very long stretch. We will discuss how it is possible to reach Mount Kailash and the Bermuda triangle later in the book. The lost city of Atlantis is said to be somewhere near Greece, and being more optimistic I would put Atlantis somewhere near the Bermuda triangle in the Atlantis Ocean. The place was imagined by Plato a Greek philosopher. Atlantis was believed to be an advanced city with a great civilization and had huge monuments, bridges and advanced canal systems. The exact period of its existence is not known but may have existed around 10,000 years before our time. Several other philosophers later also referred to the same city and interest grew but most of it may be attributed to the first mention by Plato. Mount Kailas or Kailash means the same things and sometimes if it is overlooked there may be a mention of Mount

Kailas by mistake. Kindly omit some spelling mistakes as they occur or unrecognized names as the conversion from that language to English is not exactly the same particularly for names of mountains and gods from Hindu, Chinese, Tibetan as well as other religions.

As shown in one map from 1882 the location of Atlantis is near to my assumption of it being near the Bermuda triangle. This we will discuss more in the book and if there are any links between the Bermuda triangle, Atlantis and also Mount Kailash.

Image: Lost City of Atlantis from an 1882 map. Map of the Atlantean Empire, from Ignatius Donelly's Atlantis: the Antediluvian World, 1882. (Source: Wikepedia)

Image: (Courtesy of WHOI Archives, © Woods Hole Oceanographic Institution)

The lost city of Atlantis was said to Atlantis is said to be bigger than Africa and Asia and definitely this is not possible to be located near Greece, if it was overtaken by floods or earthquakes as the area of the sea around Greece is much smaller. Neither the Asian civilizations which have some record of their history of around 5,000 to 8,000 years as per my knowledge, have no evidence of Atlantis. It is said that Mount Kailas is in the form of a pyramid and also for the Bermuda triangle, scientists have claimed to have found two glass/crystal pyramids in the ocean below water. While we are able to visit Egypt and see all of the pyramids, we do not see any magnetic attraction or other forces coming into picture in Egypt, neither do we disappear there and we do come back. But surprisingly, at Mount Kailash and Bermuda triangle people claim to have seen mysterious things happening to them which we will discuss and try to understand them.

Both Mount Kailash and the Bermuda triangle are inaccessible to science and difficult to explore with even the latest gadgets and modern technologies which include satellites, helicopters, planes, cameras, radars and other sophisticated equipment. That is why it is so interesting for everyone till someone is able to see inside it and report it to the world. Till then it is an unexplored mystery. Several expeditions to the Bermuda triangle and Mount Kailas have failed and not one has been able to unravel the mystery surrounding them. Either people get lost, disappear or something unnatural happens at Bermuda triangle and at Mount Kailash people are not able to reach the peak, abandon halfway, become old, nails and hair start to grow rapidly or even die at an early age after attempting to climb, to the peak of the mountain range. This is all that is told in hundreds of videos, the same thing is repeated in all of them and all articles and stories on the internet or in books. They tell you nothing extra except these things and stories about failed explorers and their experiences.

When I try to read something different about Mount Kailas or Bermuda triangle, I come across the same stories repeated in all of the different articles, videos and books. We have not gone beyond that even after several years have passed and much more explorations have taken place there. You need to read the entire

book to know everything I will talk about Mount Kailash and Bermuda triangle if I live alive to complete the book.

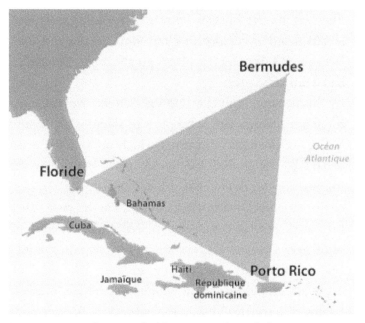

Image: Bermuda triangle (Source: Wikipedia)

Some people have related Mount Kailash to the center of the Earth and the Earth's axis and magnetic field and some even said it was a pyramid and even went further made a map or copied its shape and said it resembled the human genes. Some of them say there are several caves inside the mountain where saints and others do penance and worship. A Chinese mission is said to have gone inside the caves but they found no saints or holy people there but a rumor was spread that they got hold of several manuscripts, which again appears false as they show it as modern paper manuscripts which is highly impossible to exist in ancient times. A few said there was a hole at the top which seen from above showed alien ships inside it.

None of these rumors and stories could be verified and attempts to do recorded missions with cameras have also failed.

They say several Russian scientists who went to unravel the secrets failed to get anything and some became old and died. Whenever helicopters or planes go above the Mount Kailash bad weather

starts, similar to the one seen at the Bermuda triangle forcing the planes and helicopters to abandon their missions. While we do have submarines which explore the oceans at several places around the world, none have given us the information we need about the Bermuda triangle or the Lost city of Atlantis. That is what surprises me the most. There are private submarine companies as well which operate private tours in the oceans. You can search for them on the internet. But scientists are not willing to take the risks of the explorations and maybe the submarines are not interested in taking risks either. This is the reason the things remain a mystery forever and I have to write a book explaining everything based on available content and my knowledge similar to Plato's assumption of Atlantis.

We need to know why Mount Kailas and Bermuda triangle are inaccessible and why we can go to Mars and see everything there, we can go to the Moon see there and return but are unable to see what is there on Mount Kailas and the Bermuda triangle.

Bermuda triangle remained unexplored because whenever people tried to reach there, they either disappeared, the planes or the ships disappeared and the instruments started malfunctioning, in some cases, the planes went into a different world or shifted in time and space and reached an entirely different location instantaneously.

IMAGE: GLASS/CRYSTAL Pyramid found at Bermuda triangle below water in the ocean. They are said to be three times bigger than the Gaza and other Egyptian pyramids and exist around 2,000 meters below the surface of the water. (Source: Wikipedia)

For every mountain in the Himalayas or other places, where there are shrines or holy places, you need to Criss cross several mountains before you reach the center of the mountain ranges. I have seen this for most of the places/shrines located in the mountains. This can only be done by walking/trekking several kilometers in cold and harsh weather. Now a days helicopter service is available to a certain point from Nepal or Tibet to Mount Kailash. (Source: Google Earth)

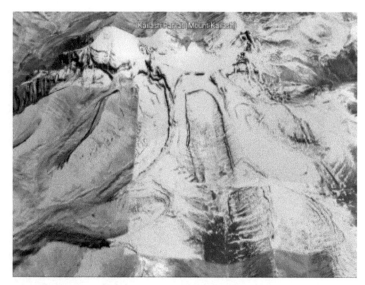

Image: Mount Kailash. View from another angle.

That is what they told not me, I have yet to see what they saw or experiences. are unable to survive in harsh weather, cloudy environment. In all of the cases the weather changed or started to change as they approached the location. Present day planes, helicopters, ships and in cyclones, thunderstorms and lightings. This is what exactly happens when the ships, planes and other travelling machines approach Bermuda triangle the weather changes here instantaneously for them. That is what I heard and read in every case and in every story of whosoever visited that periphery of the Bermuda triangle disappeared or the plane or the ship disappeared, communication went away and there was no trace of them at all.

Nothing no people, no crash, wreckage or even a communication to where they went invisible into the blue sky or the ocean ate them. Then people became afraid of the Bermuda triangle and avoided it. At times the same triangle is calm, people live in the Bermuda island nearby and also some may have visited that same location and come back also. But when they disappear there is no trace.

The reason if I tell you in the beginning, will not read the whole book and miss a lot of interesting things which need to be told about Bermuda triangle. Likewise, it is true for Mount Kailash. Whenever, we see a movie, read a story or a book we look for something interesting and if the end is told in the beginning, we are no longer interested.

Image: Location of Mount Kailash on the Map. The mountain is accessible or reachable via Kathmandu, Nepal or Lhasa, Tibet (Source: Wikipedia)

Let us go over to Mount Kailash, the same thing is repeated here, when mountaineers or ordinary people start to climb the mountain, a certain voice speaks in the mind asks them to go back and confuses their mind. The people start growing nails and hairs at a faster speed than normal and start to get older faster in maybe minutes or hours.

But those who are taking rounds around the mountain feel no such affect and feel the opposite glad and happy and achievement of a lifetime. If you were to return from Bermuda triangle alive you may also feel the same thing but sadly no one is coming alive from there.

I have visited Vaishno devi several times from childhood to adulthood and every time one goes there, he feels happy and glad on returning and a feeling of relaxation and removal of any heavy load on the mind. It is a 15 to 20 km walk up a mountain and then again coming down done by millions of people who are not mountaineers and know no rock climbing. People climb the mountain on prebuild steps and concrete roads which are along the entire stretch of 15-20 odd kilometers. It is a sacred place with a shrine at the top and as I said millions of devotees visit it every year in all seasons. The weather here is not as bad or harsh as Mount Kailash or Bermuda triangle

But at several places nearby Vaishno devi, Mount Kailash or even Bermuda triangle there are places with totally harsh environments and even in Tibet, still hundreds of people go there and somewhere there are shrines made at those locations. People travel on foot and call it hiking, after travelling on foot passing through ice, waterfalls and glaciers and even walking on the glaciers. These places however have low oxygen, old people may die due to difficulty in breathing and it is common for people to die while hiking but still you see a huge line of people climbing these peaks in the Himalayas, there are makeshift tents made of ordinary plastic with beds on these narrow and steep slopes in total rain.

Image: North face of Mount Kailash. (Source Wikipedia)

They even have food and water available while you are climbing to reach the glaciers and some remote shrine a few 40-50 kms away on a mountain which is accessible only after you pass several mountains. If you are looking for adventure and fun there are unlimited places out there and mishaps are common, it is a risk and the rate of death is the same as in accidents or living in cities these days. Places like Nepal and Tibet are now more secure for adventuring to the Himalayas and you have several places to visit to do hiking and mountaineering even as ordinary people. But you have to be careful as there are possibilities of you being looted not by dacoits but by the tour operators themselves and you should prepare all your journeys in advance from reliable tour operators rather than select small time ones who are good only for the local people. Travelling to unknown places can get you stuck. If you wish to avoid travel read this book, which will save you on the travel costs and the efforts that go with it.

In the morning everything was wonderful and we felt fresh and too much happy. There was water, a pond/stream which had stone steps which went underground for hundreds of meters. My friends told me the steps led to another city or location and wanted me to dare and attempt to go in those steps underwater, but I was afraid. I did not attempt it and neither did any of the hiking team who were with me many of them I did not know.

Even after I have walked under water when I was small child and was like a fish, did not need to breathe and could see clearly, but that was in absolutely clear water, when the water became muddy later on, I was unable to walk there in the water and had to quickly rush out of water.

Image: Full view of Mount Kailash. (Source Wikipedia)

I have stopped at places in the jungles, entered old monuments and stayed there for some time but never found anything unusual. I have felt ghosts but never seen them, ghosts have come in the night in the sleep suffocated me and even tried to finish me off several times, but when I woke up everything was ok as if nothing happened. These things happen only in the sleep or in the dreams, but are not present when we are awake. As soon as we wake up from the sleep the ghost or whatever thing it there vanishes as if it was our imagination even if it was real in the first place.

What has my experiences to do with mysteries Mount Kailash or maybe at the Bermuda triangle. I am not a very rich person and yet to succeed as a big writer, my resources to travel are limited, although I have travelled a lot but always have been on a limited budget. Had I travelled to Mount Kailas or the Bermuda triangle, I am very sure nothing would happen to me except of course accidents or maybe death for sure. So, if you think I should first visit Mount Kailash or Bermuda triangle and then write the book, it won't do any good. Neither it will do you any good if you visit those places without reading my book. Maybe reading my book may be cheaper than actually going there in the first place.

We are all humans and are not mortals as one would want to think about himself or others and it took me lot of years to realize it that I am not immortal. Even if I were to become immortal, I would not tell you about it neither to anyone in the world. That is what Mount Kailas is about people say it is.

Image: Close view of Mount Kailash. (Source Wikipedia)

After that several attempts at entering the water has been unsuccessful and I can swim only 50-100 meters the most and if the water is not clear or dirty, I feel suffocated and uneasy.

After that hiking trip on the mountain, many years later another friend of mine drowned in similar conditions visiting one such unknown place on another mountain, which I never went to but was told by my friends who survived and it also happened with another friend who lost their colleague in a similar hiking adventure.

I also visited another place which was called the birth place of Hanuman and it was also on top of a very big mountain but it was not in the Himalayas but more than 1000 kms away from it in India. There also after climbing to the peak there was a small shrine and a pond and while one of my colleagues took bath there, I kept duty on him entire time afraid of some evil happening. Even after warning him several times, he took bath there and I was in panic mode till he took the bath and came out.

With age, I have become a coward when it comes to such things as exploring the unknown, prefer to play safe and in two such cases, when taking bath in these unknown locations some creature from the water pulled me, but was saved two times.

I have even become afraid to take baths when I see ponds or water sources in these jungles and mountains unless they are poodles or just small amount of water pockets.

At one time I was not afraid of anything, maybe at that time I was quite young and would go into haunted houses, stand at graveyards in the night and walk barefoot in the jungles.

Mount Kailash is related to immortality and visiting it washes you of your entire sins and attaining heaven. I am sure after reading this many of the sinners would want to visit Mount Kailash rather than going to the Bermuda triangle. Which means even if you were to die at Mount Kailash, you feel you have a chance of going to heaven and who would not want it.

Image: Nearest airports near Mount Kailash. Some of these may be only helicopter services in some locations. (Source: Google maps)

We have seen several movies which show similar hiking done by mostly young men and women who start trekking in jungles, do similar things get drowned, are eaten by crocodiles, other wild animals and something unknown happens and they disappear, but those things do not gain as much popularity as the ones we are discussing. We start searching for them but they disappear and never reach back to civilization or their homes even after being educated and knowing their home addresses. After a brief search and depending on the amount of money we have we start to lose hope of them ever coming back and abandon the search missions. Some movies do show survivors and successful search and rescue operations.

I have wandered into the jungles aimlessly when I was a child or very young, but always came back as I marked my limit and kept a trace of my path usually using streams, and locations to remember my return paths, but still I did get lost a few times but have managed to come back.

In school I was in scouts and was also a scout's captain and we had regular trekking and hiking missions, maybe that was the reason for me venturing into forests and going mountaineering and doing explorations. I developed fear as I grew in age over the 30s and now, I am cautious and afraid to venture to the same jungles which I felt were my home when young. But in a group with young people very few old people are afraid to do hiking in the jungles.

How do we know the world was destroyed completely and rebuilt?

Mountains and seas have survived most of the impact of destruction on earth and are the most visible and prominent objects that remained the same even after several thousands of years. For every religion the mountains are sacred and several temples and shrines have been built on mountains where people climb the difficult journey just to feel happy and joyous of the achievement and get a connection to God. All pain and suffering of years go away when you visit these mountains and the shrines in them.

It is not because of the shrines that you feel happy, but the shrine is an attraction force that helps you claim the mountain. If there is no shrine and you climb the mountain or even a hill you will not feel happy or glad. You can try this experiment in a nearby hill or mountain nearby you. The hill or mountain must have a shrine or a religious connection for you to feel happy climbing it. The same is true for Mount Kailash or any other mountain with the same religious significance.

Destruction on the planet has occurred several times in last 15,000 years or more. Several destructions came on the planet and it was destroyed and build several times over again and again. History was saved and destroyed several times. Technology was made and destroyed several times.

But Technology has not always been the same. In earlier times, small ponds, mud dams, bathing places and bullock carts, horse carts and chariots were considered as technology by us. Not by the old civilizations which existed then. Over the time they even had forging, making swords, and weapons and metal parts of different types. This we consider as technology which meant they knew how to create fires, melt and purify metal also, which is a big thing by our standards.

But while we feel ours is an advanced civilization in the present, it is an advanced one no doubts about that, but the Chinese, Egyptian, Greek, Hindu, Inca and several other civilizations also knew about the stars, their orientation, they could calculate the distances between planets and they also knew other planets and star systems existed. Today NASA and all space agencies combined together do not even know one percent of all the information that the primitive tribals knew. There are several drawings and inscriptions and other representative symbols which have been left by them. Particular one is astrology and knowledge of space has been preserved although there are no written records on space, astrology and orientation and location of the star systems.

This means that people from those civilizations survived and passed on that information from generation to generation till we were able to convert it to written and digital form.

The excavations reveal to us the ancient civilizations that existed before us. Sometimes we call them as advanced civilizations even if we find some sort of dams or mechanized wooden equipment's. A complete destruction meant that the entire planet was filled with water leaving very little scope for saving everything and Earth remained submerged for several hundred years before becoming normal. Some of these destructions are mentioned by Moses and in some religious scripts. This resulted in wipe out of complete civilizations and there is no clue anyone was saved as we did not have written history.

In the last 2000 years or so, there has not been complete destruction of the civilizations as was the situation before 2000 years. We have also started to write history and preserve it in some form or another and we are taught history in schools as well. Some history has been passed to us from generation through generation from word of mouth and later converted into written form later when we started writing. We also found old texts written on wood and parched paper, which we converted into modern writing and now in digital form as well which gave us much insight into history.

Everyone on the planet is supposed to know this. Destructions happened because of several reasons and also because of seasonal changes in weather, earthquakes, volcanoes and other natural causes. But all of the planet's civilization did not disappear at once, except in one case when the entire earth was flooded with water. Some earthquakes came at some places at some time and other ones at other places at other times.

Now people survive even in earthquakes, floods, volcanoes, famines and even in painful wars and there are several reasons for that.

There are many mysteries in the world. But when I start exploring the mysteries and the superstitions that go along with them most of them have been found to be fake. After years of research the things are not as people claim to exist.

Mysteries and Magic

Before explaining to you everything about Mount Kailash and the Bermuda triangle, I will explain to you the meaning and realities of mysteries and magic. Without understanding mysteries and magic in addition to superstitions, you will never be able to know completely about Mount Kailash, Bermuda triangle and other mysterious places on Earth.

When I go in detail, I go into everything, the flesh, blood, bones, eyes, ears and even inside the blood and the organs. When I explore the mountains, aliens, spacecrafts, outer planets, I go into the mountains, caves, stones, atoms, space, time and visit all the galaxies and all of the planets as if I am there physically inside them.

For years I believed in magic and though it to be real and after seeing several of the videos and analyzing them, I ultimately found magic to be fake done with the help of several gadgets. When cameras came, everyone thought magic would die and people would be caught doing the tricks, but even now people are doing the same tricks and are able to fool the camera. Whenever there was a chance, I interacted with magicians went closer, and allowed them to use their tricks on me, but was never convinced their magic was real.

My view of magic is that if people can make things appear and disappear then they should be able to do anything instantly, but it is not so, they require very hard practice. Someone who can make book disappear cannot make other objects disappear, he can make coins disappear but cannot do with other objects such as pencils or pens.

For me magic is only true when he is able to disappear pen, pencil, book, coins everything then only it is magic. If he can guess person's name or read mind, he should be able to read mind for many other things rather than one or two names which he asks the people to remember before playing the magic trick. Most of the people hardly remember the name or object they had stored in their minds and the magician takes advantage of that.

Now everyone has heard of Mount Kailash and Bermuda triangle and these are similar to the tricks of a magician and also the superstitions we believe in. During the olden times, a few thousands of years back, the Kings, Brahmins, Sadhus, Clergy in Christians, and Mullahs in Muslims forced us to limit our minds to believe only in certain things and warned us of severe dangers or consequences should we go beyond certain limits in using our minds to read or explore about anything in and around us. Every religion had that practice.

We were not to wander at night, women were to wear certain types of clothes only and cover their headgear which was there in Hindu, Muslim as well as in Christian religions except in very poor people, who could not afford clothes. These superstitions were only in cities and well of people who had money to buy clothes and live in houses and was not applicable to all people.

These are only some of the superstitions. The other superstitions were with respect to certain temples, churches and even mosques that were considered sacred and access to them was limited and people could not visit certain rooms or locations in them. There was a set of secrecy and even today at several of these places the rooms are locked for hundreds of years with no one allowed to go and find out what is there in them. Those that are opened nothing has been found and in some of the room's gold ornaments and other precious stones and necklaces have been found in billions of dollars donated by devotees over several years hundreds of years back at the shrines.

Altogether, nothing mystic or magical or the unknown was found at these shrines. Nothing bad happened after opening those rooms, but at some places the courts have been warned that entire state or country may disappear if one or two rooms that are left in that shrine are opened, which makes even judges fear opening them to find out the mystery.

The Bermuda Triangle and mount Kalash and several other similar places remain unexplored precisely because of that reason. In certain places even policemen and other people have experienced ghosts and supernatural forces when visiting victims and have run away, unable to know if it is actual criminal activity or really ghosts at that places.

That fear factor makes it impossible to know completely about those places and till someone is actually able to reach the epicenter of that place, it remains a mystery. Those mysteries have been solved where people reached the epicenters of them and we await technologies for exploring the rest of the places which are still in the dark as to their truthfulness.

Nothing is new everything is pre-existing and will remain so, but weather and other conditions such as earthquakes, floods, famines, volcanic eruptions, other natural causes

And now wars and use of missiles, nuclear bombs and so on will keep changing civilizations and pre-existing things and overwriting them with new ones. People start imagining things and start superstitions and even go to the extent of creating existence of technologies 2,000-15,000 years back that plane, spaceships may have existed. There may have been nuclear bombs and the civilizations may have been more advanced than what we have at present and even magic existed in those times.

I neither deny nor accept those things. Even I have a problem, I feel losing my magic and even after trying very hard have not been able to restore my magical powers. But I learnt an important thing that if I had those magical powers, which I think I have it would have been misused by me several times over. Sometime I feel empty without the magic and sometimes I feel I am better off without my magical powers.

The books about magic which the people wrote, which included the Christians, Hindus well as the Muslims the themselves did not know the magic, but they wrote them just like Harry Potter or other books written in modern times and I liked reading all of them, each and every one of them including Superman, Batman, Fantom, Flash Gordon, all Arabian magic tales, all Hindu magic tales everything I read till I could read no more. But all of them gave me no magic and even after seeing magic in front of my eyes several times the tricks performed in front of me, I have never been able to replicate them in my life.

One magician took out a glass of milk from my hand, another magician climbed me on a rope in front of an audience and I was on the terrace a few moments later. In another case, magicians hypnotized everyone but I was not hypnotized and self-hypnosis did nothing to me.

But I am still waiting for the day when my magic powers return maybe when I am mature enough not to misuse them in anger. That is the only situation when I will misuse my magic powers and still believe magic exists somewhere.

Mount Kailash and the Bermuda triangle

So now we start from here and start discussing about Mount Kailash and the Bermuda triangle. While Bermuda triangle has only one name but Mount Kailash has several names, the reason is that it is the belief of several religions and is mentioned in several religions and their religious texts. The names are different because their languages, religions and culture is different. Some know it as Mount Meru (Buddhists) and some know it as Gang Rinpoche (Tibetan) and Kangrinboqe (Chinese/Tibet). Since Mount Kailash is in form of a pyramid it has three sides and represents three religions Hindu, Chines and Buddhism. By mistake I told it represents four religions and most of the people now on the internet and books relate it to four religions which then also includes Christianity. After I start using this everyone in world will accept my theory and still there is a fifth religion left which is Muslim which also may get represented with Mount Kailash if I want to change history to what I believe.

Mount Kailas represents Lord Shiva for Hindus and for others it represents different Gods. For Buddhists (Tibetans) it represents Buddha and for Jains who are from India it

represents the abode of Mahavir and the several rebirths of
Mahavir who has the same form as Buddha but is different
from him in form and in history. I know everything but will
be unable to write it, as I told your body and the spinal cord
pains badly converting my mind database to actual books. I am
only able to write when the mind is hyperactive and then it tells
me everything I should write and I have to do it as quickly as
possible before I feel tired and leave the book unfinished. After
that it is as if I know nothing. Mount Kailas also represents the
Bon religion which existed predominately in the 11th Century
in Tibet and is now in a minority. In short, Mount Kailas
represents several religions including the Chinese religion.
Tibetans also refer to Mount Kailash as the abode of God Dem
Chok(omit spellings here).

I can write everything about each of these Gods but maybe
later or at the end of the book of possible. But first priority is
to write about Mount Kailash and the Bermuda Triangle and if
they are interlinked.

Hindus are very strong in their beliefs and even I am a
Hindu, but I believe strongly in all religions. Except the Quran,
I have read almost all other religions including the Vedas, Bible,
Testament and other holy books. Maybe I may read the Quran
also at some period of time.

I know the sacredness of every holy book and also the
unread ones, they have the same thing in them about an eternal
God and some have prophets of God who pass on messages of
God to us from time to time.

Some of the Gods and Prophets include Moses, Jesus,
Muhammad, Krishna, Ram, Buddha, Mahavir and several
others who passed on the same message to different religions

with exactly the same things and same teachings on which we made our holy books which are the constitution of every individual religion and their prophets and gods.

We look to them as our ideals and life started when we were brought here on this planet and different religions describe things differently to us, how we came to be here on Earth.

For me everyone on Earth is a robot, a self-operated one who has a mind like a computer and his body parts are similar to that of an advanced robot which will come into a similar human form in the 23rd century around 200 years from now, if life on Earth does not become extinct. These robots made of metal will be similar to what we are today and do exactly what we do today except they will require energy in form of batteries or electricity to run. That is what makes us different from robots. This will be made possible with artificial intelligence which we are developing. Neither robot is immortal, neither humans can be immortal.

Let us come to the main topic if the book again. Hindus regard Mount Kailas as the abode of Lord Shiva and other religions regard it as the abode of their gods respectively as Buddha, Mahavir, Dem Chok ((omit spellings here).

All the religions have different languages and their gods look different and are not having identical faces but reside at the same location of Mount Kailas which if it is a pyramid has three directions and are sacred to India, Nepal, China and Tibet as understood in the first phase.

Even if Mount Kailas has relation to the Christian religion as well as the Muslim religion, I will not elaborate on it, neither want any religion offended on it. A rumor exist that Lord

Jesus had visited the Himalayas at the same place in Mount Kailas and stayed there since I told you I read extensively on everything on Earth. But there is no such thing I read on Prophet Muhammad having visited Mount Kailash.

Sometimes to make their books popular many authors spread such rumors to popularize their books by making controversial statements of something which cannot be proved. As I tell in all my books related to religion and existence of life and nature, God is universal, appears different to different religions and it is like a garden which has different flowers. Co-incidentally, Mount Kailash or Mount Meru is also a representation of different religions, the God maybe the same but he cannot be worshipped in the same form by all religions. This will happen one day when superstitions go away and people are more ready to accept each other's religions and do not think different from each other.

Sometimes, I want one universal religion and sometimes I feel that people are much better off as different religions. Those are secrets which can never be told to you as I am no prophet of God. It is too much damaging and destructive to have one single religion as it is to have only one type of flower in the world or we have only one type of fruit or vegetable.

Everyone would become a robot if we have one religion and no one wants to be a robot. I wanted people to communicate on the internet to reduce travel and save on petrol, but travel has increased and so has the number of cars and vehicles. Then after COVID-19 came, I felt now that it was possible for all to work remotely, but after COVID-19, ended now travel is the same or more than before. I though emails would reduce courier and postage, but nothing has reduced now we have more parcels from shopping sites than postal mails. The variety has increased and not decreased. Similarly, when we have robots, humans are not going to be displaced. People have not got displaced when computers came and even after having so many technological advancements, we still do not know anything about Mount Kailash or the Bermuda triangle.

You will argue that how is my above paragraph have anything to do with finding out the secrets of Mount Kailash or Bermuda triangle. I want to say that even if tomorrow we have sophisticated robots who can climb Mount Kailash still it may not be possible to unravel the mystery of either Mount Kailash or the Bermuda triangle. Many of the things on Mars or our Moon were a secret till we had missions which showed us there was nothing there of use to us except adventure.

The Mount Kailas like situations are there on our Moon and on Mars as well. Travel to Mars gave us nothing, it is just an empty barren land where even vegetation cannot grow. The Moon has a very harsh atmosphere and even after it takes only 2-4 days to reach there, we abandoned the Moon missions. The only things we collected from the Moon were a few stones which appear to be different and analysis of those rocks gave us nothing. There is no diamond or gold on the Moon to mine either which would make it lucrative and an incentive for us to send more missions.

Venus and Mercury are hot, so they are ruled out for explorations but for Venus, still missions are being planned. We have had Venus, Mars, Saturn and Jupiter moon missions completed but for Venus and Jupiter's moon they were only on the outside with no landings. The Mars missions are now landed non-human missions and no life has been found there. We are yet to see any unknown thing like the Bermuda triangle or Mount Kailash at Mars or any other planet.

There are rumors that the Moon missions were abandoned as the astronauts had the same experiences as the Bermuda triangle and Mount Kailash where they were warned to stay off the Moon. While space agencies are trying to send human missions to Mars, it does not seem practicable at the moment when it is so difficult to send astronauts to space station and bring them back.

But nothing can be said about the future and technologies can change and we may have better options then. We don't have a Bermuda triangle situation on our Moon, Mars or Venus as we are not having any sea or ocean there.

We have found out that Bermuda triangle is an area in the Atlantic Ocean which is part of an old civilization called the Atlantis which got drowned in the ocean thousands of years back during the time of Moses. In addition to the Atlantic city there were several other civilizations which also drowned at the same time as the flooding occurred on the entire Earth.

According to Moses, God had warned of the flooding of the Earth to Moses, who passed it on to the ones who believed in him. He makes a huge Ark, a boat of wood, collected all types of animals and as much as possible humans, which included men, women, and children and took them to a high mountain where they survived. After several months or years when the waters settled back to the oceans and seas, the people came down and settled and spread all over the Earth again, rebuilding themselves.

Everything on Mars seems to be destroyed as I saw from all of the explorations and from what I could imagine, there is no trace of life and it appears there were several explosions all over the planet all of which were either nuclear or atomic bombs exploding resulting in Mars being what it is today.

The same thing would have happened in the Russia-Ukraine war which is happening today. I took a lot of steps to avert the nuclear war and the president of Russia threatened to bomb the entire world with nuclear and atomic bombs. My contributions will not be recognized till the countries themselves US and Europe say it was my indirect intervention which prevented the fallout. My book on Mars (Mystical Mars) was written much before the Russia-Ukraine war and it already said everything about Mars having been destroyed due to an atomic or nuclear war.

Still, we are interested in exploring Mars, even after it has been destroyed and nothing exists there and all of the water and air has been eaten up by the nuclear explosions which took hundreds of years to settle, like Hiroshima and Nagasaki nuclear explosions in the World War II.

Similar destructions have occurred on Earth although I do not see any kind of nuclear explosions having occurred on Earth before Hiroshima and Nagasaki but as I said the occurred to floods, famines, earthquakes and volcanoes.

That is why we see remains of several civilizations under the ground and also under the sea waters at all places on Earth in all the continents and countries. The remains of the monuments and artifacts underground and in in the seas and oceans means that the civilizations did not perish due to nuclear explosions or due to even use of ordinary gun powder. Stone structures are found to be intact and without any marks of severe damage on them.

Adventure and Thrill

Most of the places we visit or want to visit is out of adventure and thrill. Some people live trekking and hiking and some love to see new places. Some want to be excited and some just want to go away from all the stress and burden of city life. One thing we see is when we move away far from our place of stay whether it is a city or a village, we tend to become stress free. The reason is that lot of things are on our minds when we stay at the same place for a very long time.

The consciousness is interrelated in a particular city or location even in a village where we are living for some years or an entire lifetime. We need to get away from this single monotonous and boring activity. Visiting religious places, tourist spots, resorts, jungles, mountains and unknown places gives us relief from stress and depression of a regular life in our home place. We also get to know new things and get sheer pleasure out of it.

Religion is an attraction which forces us to visit those places which are impossible to visit in normal mind. Most of these places are in mountains and in jungles where it is impossible to go under normal circumstances, but at the same time thousands of people are going to them which makes them safe as we have people all around us. So if you are visiting a holy place in a mountain range where you have to either travel, climb several mountains or cross several glaciers, you find it less difficult as in the entire route there are tents, food, people around you and also people staying at several junctions on the entire route.

If by chance there were on tents. Hotels, food and people along with you on the entire route to these shrines and holy places you would never be able to go there. At these remote locations these people survive also single handedly with very less support and food. This is the adventure and the thrill and on return you feel a sense of achievement and excitement of having got something very valuable.

This is similar to the experiences you have while going on a holiday to a tourist place or another city or country. For your entire lifetime you tend to recall the event many times over till old age.

History of Mankind

The history of humans is not millions of years old as claimed by scientists and it is brainwashing of humans.

WRITING WAS INVENTED hardly 1500-2000 years ago. Scientists claim fossils are millions of years old and only bacteria lived on Earth, but we have not seen life on any other planet in our solar system and neither is life there in any other solar system or galaxy.

We have not been able to find even one other solar system while we are able to see galaxies hundreds of light years away, but we cannot see any solar system which are actually nearer to us. Only I know the reason but it is not the right time to tell. How can fossils be millions of years old when we have no trace of forts, kingdoms, kings more than 2000-5000 years as on date.

All of our recorded history is only 2000-5000 years back and all artifacts, historical monuments, excavations of human built monuments are hardy a few thousands of years old.

Every human, animal, bird, fish, and any other life forms
have the same body structures. They all have cells and their
body shapes are in exactly similar pattern for a particular type.
Therefore, neither the dinosaurs are more than 5000 years old.

Even if life was destroyed during the time of Moses and
entire planet was covered with floods, then also there would
have been leftover remains of forts, temples, monuments and
other evidences left. But nothing was left even after the great
flood and there are no traces of earlier civilizations also.

While I have claimed that there is a hot core in every planet
and then there a number of layers above that core, then the
seas and the Artic and the Antarctic regions help to keep the
planet cool, but when we see Mars, it has no water still it is not
as hot as it should be. Its Artic and Antarctic region is almost
destroyed and has only carbon gases. So how does Mars remain
cool even without the huge oceans and seas we are having.

But we have seen Earth is extremely hot and has deserts in
places where there is very less or no water, but we do not have
deserts on Venus or Mercury. There may be deserts on those
planets, but they have not yet been found although hot lava
may have been discovered.

Now we are having the James Web Telescope sending us
lots and lots of images of the Universe. But you see the
Universe is very large and when we see the images from the
James Web Telescope, we see lot of shapes of animals like cats,
dogs, horses and also shapes of human beings in them. These
images seem untrue and unbelievable. The images are not
actually taken by the Telescope but are generated using infrared
technology as there is no science or equipment available which

can see those images in the first place from such a large distance.

To take images in space for very large distances such as millions of years, we can only use infrared light rays and not ordinary light. The cameras in our houses and in computers use ordinary light to decipher images and whatever light reflects back we convert them to images using technology.

We cannot send light to far away objects millions of light years away and get their reflections back, neither can we absorb light from far away objects and capture them and convert them to images. That is why we cannot decipher long distance images.

Ultimately, the only surprising thing is that the space probes were able to send us images using radio frequency such as the Voyager space probes.

A SPACE PROBE IS JUST like a satellite, which instead of moving around the planet like Earth moves out into deep space, so you get same type of data we are getting from artificial satellites moving around Earth which give us news, weather information and transmit internet data and videos and other information about planet Earth.

Diversion to different topics is to make the book interesting and also let you more about science. For me I always wonder why science is so behind in discovering secrets of Mountain Kailash, Lost City of Atlantis and Bermuda Triangle. It always surprises me with so much advanced technology, we are still blind and worse than ancient stone age in technology.

The Indus valley has baffled scientists, but one forgets that at that time Alexander had invaded India and the time of existence of the Indus valley and Harappan Civilizations almost match with Alexander's invasion of India at that time. In almost all probability, it was that invasion which may have destroyed the Harappan and Indus Valley Civilizations.

While those civilizations are considered as advanced, we forget that there were hundreds of such civilizations existing across the length and breadth of the world which were also having similar types of structures and systems of drainage, which the Indus and Harappan civilizations had and those monuments and their canal systems are still in existence today. There are the Incas and also in Peru lot of advances canal and drainage systems as well as in other countries which are having much stronger material of construction such as in the Lost City of Atlantis.

The Lost City of Atlantis has several such canals and drainage systems and also bridges. But obviously bridges have been existing for a very long time, otherwise how was it possible for our ancestors to cross big rivers and conquer unknown lands and countries.

History of Mankind is unlimited as there were hundreds of civilizations and each claimed it was influenced by Gods from another planets or galaxies. When I got to know that Earth was actually a prison where people from different galaxies are sent here because they are considered lazy and like music, dance, acting and something that is prohibited in other planets, I feel it as some kind of a joke. They say the other galaxies and planets are advanced and people work more like robots, just go to work and come back and eat in between. That is what we are slowly reaching now. Earlier we spent only a few hours working five days a week, slowly our working hours have increased to compensate for more taxes on us, then now we even have some of us working on Saturdays and Sundays. We hardly have time for pleasure and even after having lot of gadgets, internet, tv, news we are not even able to go for a normal morning or evening walk, that is how we are stressed out from work.

All these stress collects in us, and it gets off when we holiday or escape from routine work. Where do we put oof all this stress is by diverting ourselves to dance, music, painting, watching news, unexpected events and attending ceremonies such as marriage and other things.

Imagine if we had none, as they say exists in other planets and galaxies, none of these traditions, life would be very boring. But of course, it is not the truth as if rituals did not exist in other planets and galaxies, we would not be having them written in the holy books, neither would we have kings promoting art and culture and dance and music in the olden days and artists earning multiple times than us.

In ancient times, there was no way to know if a place was holy or interesting. But some person from this place reached the civilizations below and told them about this holy or interesting place and swarms of people started trekking these high-altitude places such as Mount Kailash. Not only this, there are several other places high up in the mountains where people trek every year just by spread of word of mouth without any radio communication or news or media in the olden days.

The information on the place also appeared in religious texts which were thousands of years old. These religious texts also got distributed around the entire country by God knows which means either verbal or in writing.

Olden texts were preserved by word of mouth by the saints as they said there was no writing existing and if a saint or a brahmin knew a religious text he would pass on his entire brain to another in ashrams which were like olden day schools. Some brahmins did it with passing on the knowledge of religious texts to their children until when writing came, it got converted into text. The text is still complicated enough not to be understood by other human beings and needs lots of translations which different religious saints consider in different ways, no one has the same opinion about the same text.

When I see the different languages, I always imagine who difficult those languages are. They are puzzling, still the brains of the Indians, Chinese, Arabs, Serbians, French, Thailand people still understand and read and write them, which are almost impossible for me to write or read unless I was born there or lived there for number of years.

My name in Chinese comes like this:

◇◇◇◇

Jiǎ gé dí shén

No amount of logic I apply makes me figure out how my name is written in Chinese.

In Punjabi it is:

◇◇◇◇◇◇

Although, by birth I am a Punjabi, still it is hard to figure out my name in both languages. All these people whether the Chinese, Hindus, Christians, Thai, Incas, Mesopotamians, Greeks, Egyptians all of them spoke languages, they spoke them for hundreds of years since they came to Earth or were born here. Which means they knew how to write. How else would the language symbols exist in the first place. For speaking the language, one can understand it is transferred from parent to child, but then to understand the writings one also needs to have access to the language alphabets/symbols.

This means writing existed since mankind or human beings came into existence and there was no stone age theory. Because if we were into a stone age then why would different languages exist. Neither have the languages changed since thousands of years neither their symbols and alphabets have changed. The languages also did not disappear like dinosaurs disappeared from Earth unless the entire civilizations disappeared. But even after death of complete civilizations their writings still exist.

So ultimately, we have been built by aliens and preprogrammed with different languages to give us different identities much like we have different types of plants and flowers and animals. But our masters whom we call Gods stay hidden from us as they say, we cannot see them while we are alive and can only see them after death.

These mysterious places are also like this, their mysteries will remain unknown to us till we are alive, unless someone returns from the death and tells it to us, which is highly impossible.

Shangri-la

Shangri-La is a mysterious city supposed to be situated under mount Kailas. This city is said to be assessable only by meditation. I am a poor meditator as whatever time I have spent in meditation; I hardly gain anything except vast knowledge, which I write them in books. No Shangri-La for me.

Shangri-La is a mysterious city which has all the pleasures of life and most of the intelligent people of the world live there and the city is much the same and mysterious like the Lost city of Atlantis in vastness and in technology.

The details of Shangri-La are mentions in Tibetan texts in the first place and also have some mention in the Hindu texts, Buddhist texts and in other texts. How different religions add the same information is beyond me at present will leave it later for discussion. All of them mention Shangri-La as the heaven and some even mention it as 2400 to 2800 km long, big enough for all our satellites and planes and radars to detect them. But unfortunately, our science seems to be primitive, can see nothing.

Even after James Web Telescope saw everything in the Universe which include stars, galaxies, cats, dogs, horses, humans bigger than several planets and galaxies as lot of you may have seen the live pictures of the telescope is beaming, it cannot see what is on Earth.

Shangri-La is a city where humans like us live either in the live state or as ghosts, which in all probability is true as religious texts and learned saints swear by it as maybe they can see them or saints from the dead have contacted the live saints and told them about this city, asked them to meditate and come to this place after death or when alive.

The inquisitiveness to obtain an entry pass to this city grows out of the description given by the religious text or the learned saint, who himself did not get a chance for the entry pass to this city as alive or dead. Those who hear him or read the religious texts also want to meditate to reach the city as alive or death.

In our times people want to go to Mount Kailas, Lost city of Atlantis and Bermuda Triangle in the same ways as some want to go to Shangri-La.

The James Web Telescope shows lot of different imaginaries using its infrared technology to create actual images of what could exist in those far away galaxies, stars and the planets. While it was very successful in making those images using infrared, we could not see any aliens or any interiors of the planets such as houses, buildings, rivers and the oceans and the seas. While such a thing should have been possible for the telescope to see, at least for the nearest Andromeda galaxy of not for far away galaxies.

Neither was the telescope able to see anything or identify any nearby solar systems which would have given us more details of nearby life. Our technology is itself mysterious, it cannot detect nearby objects neither identify them from inside, but the technology can only see far away objects which are actually of no use to us. Spy satellites can see in other countries with live shows, but have no means to see things in their own countries. Therefore, mysteries continue to remain mysteries because we want them to remain mysteries and it is left to the trekkers and explorers to untangle the mysteries rather than technology helping them to do it. The explorer or the trekker also uses his hands and feet to explore rather than using advanced gadgets and means to find out more about the mysterious places with limited resources at his disposal.

When we see images made by James Web Telescope using its infrared technology, we are actually seeing outdated images as the light from these images was transmitted millions of years back. For example, the galaxies are billions of miles away from us presently and when they transmit light using their own Sun it takes time to travel at speed of light which is 3×10^8 m/s (The distance travelled by light in one second in meters).

Any light transmitted by any Galaxy or a Star is actually reaching us after 2.5 million years. We therefore do not know the present state of the galaxy or the star even if we get those images.

Tomorrow if we were to develop a technology to see those images, we still would not have a current information and since our life is at the most 60-100 years the information would almost be useless or just like an adventure of a sort.

WHEN I HAD DIED ALL, I could see me was in a small air bubble travelling faster than light or maybe at the speed of light. My travel was very fast and I got afraid and came back instantaneously not wanting to leave the planet. The number of times I wanted to go back I failed to repeat death. When I was in space for a few seconds I was very afraid came back instantaneously and whenever I want to go back to space and stand there, it is impossible for me to repeat it again. All I could see was darkness all around and it was warm and not cold, briefly I saw a planet cannot say which planet it was but it was big and I returned.

So, I know that space travel is possible without spacecrafts and it is possible inside the body but can be done only after death or if it repeats with me what happened and I still remain alive after moving out of the body and come back quickly. I have tried to repeat those incidents but have not been very successful.

There are lot of planes after death and no one knows where he will go whether he will go to Shangri-La or go to heaven. These are the imaginary planes similar to the ones we see in the dreams or called realms. That is why we should never see death and never try to experiment with death. Once, we see death in life, it pulls us towards it like a magnet. Death is a powerful magnet which is impossible to avoid if we see it before the end of life.

That is what saints do try to encounter death while living and all of their live is spent in trying to communicate with death when alive. Our object is only to worship God for the only purpose of worship and not to see him when alive. The thousands of images from James Web Telescope will not show us where God is as he can be seen only after death. Neither visiting Mount Kailas or the Bermuda Triangle or the Lost City of Atlantis can we see God when alive.

Instruments and cameras have taken entire pictures of Mars and maybe even Jupiter, Uranus, Neptune and Pluto but even there we could not see Gods or aliens or any other form of life. We invented the Hubble and the James Web Telescope still we could not see aliens or Gods. Then will it be possible for us to see anything in Mount Kailas, Bermuda Triangle or the lost City of Atlantis except ancient ruins.

God has not banned us from seeing galaxies, stars and far away planets either using telescopes or using spacecrafts or using satellites. Then why would he ban us from seeing what is inside Mount Kailas, Bermuda Triangle or the Lost City of Atlantis unless they contain ghosts. Those places can be called as haunted places rather than any mysterious powers holding us back from seeing what is in them in the first place.

Even if at some later date, if we were to find out what is in them, all the haunting would go away and we would just be walking in them like we roam around in ruins of ancient civilizations whose remains can still be seen in Egypt and other places.

Similarly, the galaxies, stars and even Mars will be a haunted place much like the Moon which is also a haunted place, unfit for humans to stay there. If and when humans stay on the Moon or on Mars, they would be living in a haunted atmosphere full of fear for the first few expeditions. That is why we visit haunted places for the thrill of it and to see after live closer. But as technology develops, we still will be able to live in space like we stay in space stations and more of us are there on

Mars and the Moon. That will take lot of time and we will need to pay a lot of taxes for our scientists to get there and send us that information.

Our taxes would have been much lower had we no space missions and less research on space and technology and we would have been living a much peaceful live with more time for pleasure and family.

Whatever extra we are paying is for technology, and as needs of the technology and research grow, we will be paying more and more taxes till we reach and dead end where we can pay no more taxes. That is how the Roman civilization ended and that is how many of our ancient civilizations ended as people reached the end in paying taxes. Both research and technology require money and scientists require money to do research and buy and make equipment's and countries pile up huge debts on them while showing healthy balance sheets in front but with huge loans at the back.

The expenditure will go in increasing when we do the Mars missions and also spend on some permanent human colony on the Moon.

The Chinese had observatories high up in some mountain or a big hill from where they watched the stars and the planets. Everything of them was related to the gods, not only them but even the Korean, Thai, Vietnam people and of other countries had the same things the planets, stars and galaxies were related to Gods and they knew much more than us about the stars and planets then we know after spending trillions of dollars in research on space. They did not even have any instruments and we also say they did not know how to write or read and neither they had places to write the information and they did not write on the cave walls also.

Some writings are seen on the cave walls but they do not match with any known language we know today in all of the religions we have at present.

Some of the Hindu text such as the Vedas have this information without any observatory. They never build planes, spacecrafts ever but had some religious text having information about making Vimanas or aircrafts or spacecrafts. The unique thing was that the aircraft had mirrors which were built from vegetables. As I started reading, I got amazed that spacecraft parts were to be built using different types of vegetables as they had only those materials at that time.

I was more surprised as in the epics the Ramayana and the Mahabharata, they had extensively used metals in weapons and swords and in making chariots they used wood and metal.

While the stars have been constant since so many centuries or even thousands of years, the James Web Telescope and scientific theories claim that stars are not static in space and not even the galaxies are static.

But from the time of prediction of the birth of Jesus Christ to the North Star pointing to him and the birth of Lord Krishna which was pre-predicted to happen. While the birth of Lord Krishna had no link with any star, it was the astrologers who predicted his birth according to movement of stars and collection in a particular constellation and also was the story of Jesus was related to the North star. The star actually guided the wise men to Jesus which means the star specially moved from place to place in the sky for Jesus. As we all know the star is not a simple thing it is very big just like our Sun, but it moved to guide a few wise men to where Jesus was born.

What is interesting is not the movement of the North star, but the ancient people those many hundreds or a few thousands of years back knew about stars and their movements. They did not need NASA or hundreds of billions of dollars of government funds to shows movements of stars or huge telescopes, they could tell with the eye.

But now humans have become outdated, astrologers have forgotten astrology, they just read old books, no calculations are being done today everything is computerized for prediction. Still, it cannot predict the birth of Lord Jesus or Lord Krishna.

Has our technology upgraded or now we are much more dependent on machines to do science and space exploration for us. Even writing articles, essays and books are becoming computerized with no need for humans to write. People will just be reading gibberish content as all content is supposed to be non-plagiarized. So human authors like us may vanish over a period of time as science and artificial intelligence advances.

I myself work in artificial intelligence, we get paid very low in 0.01 cents per task and now with age cannot do these AI tasks as it puts pressure on the heart as we prepare these AI queries to be used by machines and robots later in the same way we human work with our minds. The robots and machines will have the same limitations we humans have in future as they are made, the robots will see distant stars, not us. They will see and travel to unlimited places in space much like our space probes and Mars mission spacecrafts do.

The aliens also do the same things, if they do exist at all, they are doll plastic bodies filled with artificial intelligence and their masters who can be called the Gods cannot travel in space as space is cold and icy impossible for them to survive.

Most of the things I write in the books is because the books are permanent and my information will be there for a very long time to come. Coming back to the James Web Telescope the images that the telescope generates is using mass spectrograph which is a technology used to identify atoms and molecules. I am unable to figure out how a mass spectrograph can convert graphical data to images but maybe there is some new technological development not known to me.

As most of you have seen ECG or Electro cardio graph which is similar to a mass spectrograph the ECG shows our heart beats up and down in the form of a wave. This gives us an idea of if our hear is performing normal or abnormal.

Not even the doctors know how to read an ECG, it is the operator who tells the doctor, since the doctor cannot see in the heart what is the problem there. in a mass spectrograph molecules and atoms get identified which gives is the composition of the fuel or crude oil as one example of use of mass spectrograph. While writing I have to go and check if what I am writing is correct, as I have also worked as a QA auditor, so have to double check what I write is correct. Indeed, finding composition of petroleum products is done by mass spectrograph. We won't need to double check about ECG, it should be correct also.

When I assume anything about the Universe, the planets, stars, galaxies and what is there on Mars, Venus, Jupiter, Uranus or Pluto I assume it is correct as I can never go on those planets except using the out of body method in which I am not very successful as I get afraid staying out of my body after a few seconds. Now with age that power is also lost and I cannot even move a few meters out of my body except in dreams.

The James Web Telescope may also be using a combination of ECG and mass spectrograph to analyze and generate images of planets, stars, and galaxies in the same way that is done by ECG type instruments which generate graph on paper. The James Web Telescope is not an independent project by NASA but a combined project of NASA, European Space Agency and the Canadian Space agency who supplied the different components and instruments on the telescope.

Knowledge dies when you and overconfidence and knowledge can kill you as well as it can make you mad. Exploration should be limited or distributed over a large number of scientists. When you see Stephen Hawking, he already could see what the James Web Telescope is seeing now. That was because of his out of body experiences, the brain damage he had resulted in his coming in contact with the outer world in the same way I travel out of my body and come back.

The aliens or the gods travel in much the same way they can go places millions and billions of miles apart with that out of body experience and do not actually travel with their bodies and bodies need food and suitable temperature to survive.

We are still not robots and to become robots it may take a long time. Our body has limited functions and we cannot live in extreme temperatures. Mount Kailas has extreme temperatures and hardships during travel but we are able to travel there at least. But in space we cannot travel that easily and food is a problem.

It is said that Mount Kailash, Bermuda Triangle and the lost city of Atlantis have a relation with extra-terrestrial life. That is what attracts us as we think we get a chance to see something which would be a similar experience of travelling in space.

Mount Kailash is considered one of the most sacred mountains in the world by several major religions, including Hinduism, Buddhism, Jainism, and the Bon religion of Tibet. It is believed to be the abode of gods and deities, and many religious texts and ancient scriptures mention it as a place of spiritual significance. The aura of holiness surrounding the mountain adds to its mystery and attracts countless pilgrims and seekers from different parts of the world. Mount Kailash has a distinctive four-sided symmetrical shape, which makes it stand out from the surrounding mountains. This unique geological formation has contributed to various myths and legends about the mountain's origin and significance.

Shambala or Shangri-La is often described as a hidden or mythical kingdom of great wisdom, peace, and enlightenment. Here are some key aspects associated with the legendary kingdom of Shambhala:

The concept of Shangri-La appears in ancient texts and teachings, including the Kalachakra Tantra, a prominent Buddhist tantra. It is believed to have originated in ancient Indian and Tibetan traditions.

Shangri-La is often described as a hidden or mystical land, inaccessible to ordinary mortals. Its precise location is elusive and sometimes depicted as being in the Himalayan or Central Asian region. In some interpretations, it is considered an inner or spiritual realm rather than a physical place.

Shangri-La is said to be ruled by enlightened kings or rulers known as Chakravartins. These rulers possess great wisdom, compassion, and spiritual powers. They are believed to uphold moral and just governance, ensuring harmony and prosperity within the kingdom.

Shangri-La is associated with profound spiritual teachings and practices, aimed at attaining enlightenment and liberation. It is considered a place of advanced spiritual knowledge and wisdom, where esoteric teachings and practices are preserved and passed down.

Shangri-La is often associated with prophecies that predict a future era of great upheaval and chaos in the world. It is believed that during this time, the teachings of Shangri-La will become more accessible, and the kingdom will manifest in the physical world, bringing about a period of peace, enlightenment, and spiritual transformation.

Beyond its literal interpretation, Shangri-La holds symbolic meaning as an inner journey or state of consciousness. It represents an idealized state of spiritual awakening and the pursuit of a harmonious and enlightened society.

While space is not for everyone, the Bermuda Triangle, Mount Kailas and the location of Atlantis are reachable to us. Thousands visit Mount Kailash each year but no one has found the mystery behind it.

Shangri-La is more of a spiritual world an after-life sort of thing and those who have seen afterlife can understand some of it. Many have had bad experiences of afterlife and the encounter daemons rather than the actual spiritual space. The afterlife is the spirits or soul world and that is where everyone is supposed to reach after death. We are not having a body in that place and there is similar greenery and peace all around and it is similar to a resting place similar to an old aged luxurious home.

The concept of whether we remember everything after death is a mystery. I remembered everything and momentarily was out of my body travelling to the unknown soul world and in some time, I was back on my body but I felt that my memory was still with me in the travel part although I was more focused on where I was going to reach.

People relate dreams with afterlife and dreams have nothing to do with Shangri-La or afterlife. Based on our experiences in the real world with actual physical bodies our mind plays tricks on us and generates images of happenings. Sometimes it is also possible nearby left souls try to contact our minds in sleep.

When something is impossible to guess or find out we call it a mystery as science has no answer. In the dreams even living people appear exactly as they are and a story occurs where we are either eating with them, having an argument or settling a score, something is being snatched and other events similar to what occur in real life. All images are rendered exactly, the hands, feet, mouth, face and all of it including the furniture, surroundings get created in our mind during the dreams instance.

The important thing is how is the mind able to create all of those objects about which we hardly remember anything about and how is it able to contact those living souls be it our friends or relatives who are still alive and present in this physical world and then we suddenly wake up when we become conscious that we are in that movie room created by our own mind. We always wake up in the dream at the last moment when we are aware or conscious that during the entire sleep of 5-10 hours our mind was not in sleep but was playing dream movies.

The entire sleep process is dreaming and as soon as we become aware we wake up and are able to see only the last part of the dream. The rest of the dream vanishes and we can't remember any of it except the last few scenes before we wake up either due to our urinary bladder getting filled up or a normal morning wake up or an outside noise or disturbance.

The more we try to remember the dream the more it disappears from our mind. It won't allow us to remember it back. Most of the people in this world call it the sub-conscious mind something at the back. As we become more conscious due to scientific developments our bodies are the same, they have never advanced like science and I don't want them to advance like science either. The bodies are the same like they were 5000-10,000 years back with the same mind structure, the same sub-conscious mind and the same soul structure whatever.

But this outdated body and mind can still read and see thousands of videos and text over a period of time and store it no matter how vast it is. That is the beauty of one-time creation which has never been modified or changed even after thousands of years. We now even find that animals can speak languages if they are taught as seen in parrots and also experimented by some in dogs and cats. Slowly over time we may have many animals speaking as we advance in time.

Animals or humans cannot speak unless they are taught and are just empty brains at the time of birth but when educated can speak any language as we have seen a Chinese, Indian or any other can speak English and vice versa if taught that language.

Back to the mysteries of Mount Kailas. It is not the only mountain which is worshiped there are several others like it. Mount Kailash has been associated with several mysterious happenings and unexplained phenomena, often fueled by the mountain's spiritual significance and remote location. Not all will be able to see them as it depends on time of occurrence and you or me being there. Mysteries attract us and that is why we go there to these mysterious places to see an experience of a lifetime as we see them in movies.

Some visitors and pilgrims have reported witnessing unusual lights or glows around Mount

Kailash, especially during certain times of the year. These sightings have led to speculation about the presence of mystical energies or divine manifestations.

Mount Kailash's rugged and challenging terrain, coupled with its spiritual aura, has led to stories of people mysteriously disappearing in the area. However, it's essential to recognize that many of these disappearances can be attributed to the region's extreme weather conditions, difficult terrain, and lack of modern infrastructure.

Despite several mountaineering attempts in the past, Mount Kailash's summit has never been officially climbed to its peak. The mountain is considered off-limits for climbing due to its sacredness in multiple religious traditions.

Many pilgrims and visitors to Mount Kailash report feeling a strong sense of spiritual presence or an otherworldly atmosphere while in the vicinity of the mountain. Some describe experiencing a deep sense of peace, heightened awareness, or a feeling of being in the presence of divine energy.

Lake Mana Sarovar, located near Mount Kailash, is renowned for its mirror-like surface. Some believe that this phenomenon is a reflection of the spiritual purity and divine energy of the mountain.

The unique geological formation of Mount Kailash, with its symmetrical shape, has led to various mystical interpretations and legends about the mountain's origin.

Mount Kailash is home to vast glaciers and eternal snows, which have also inspired stories and myths about the mountain's eternal and timeless nature.

In comparison to Mount Kailas, the Bermuda Triangle, also known as the Devil's Triangle, is a region in the western part of the North Atlantic Ocean, bordered by points in Florida, Bermuda, and Puerto Rico. It has various unexplained disappearances of ships and aircraft within its boundaries. Many of the incidents have been attributed to known causes, still the Bermuda Triangle continues to be a subject of fascination and speculation. Some of the mysterious happenings associated with the Bermuda Triangle include:

Disappearance of ships, airplanes, and their occupants without a trace while passing through the Bermuda Triangle. The disappearances have led to theories about strange and inexplicable phenomena responsible for swallowing vessels and aircraft.

Pilots and sailors have reported experiencing unexplained electronic malfunctions, compass deviations, and communication disruptions while navigating through the Bermuda Triangle. These anomalies have led to suggestions of unusual magnetic or electromagnetic disturbances.

Some theories propose the existence of time warps or vortexes within the Bermuda Triangle that can cause sudden and inexplicable shifts in space and time, leading to mysterious disappearances.

The Bermuda Triangle is known for its unpredictable and rapidly changing weather patterns. Some theories suggest that unusual weather phenomena, such as rogue waves or waterspouts, could be responsible for the reported incidents.

Witnesses have described witnessing mysterious lights or glows hovering over the water in the Bermuda Triangle. These lights have been attributed to unidentified flying objects (UFOs) or other unexplained phenomena.

In some cases, vessels and aircraft that have disappeared within the Bermuda Triangle were not able to send out distress signals or emergency calls, raising questions about sudden and unexpected events.

Many feel that the stories and incidents associated with the Bermuda Triangle have been exaggerated or fabricated over time, adding to the mystery and misconceptions about the region.

It's important to note that while the Bermuda Triangle has captured public imagination and sparked various conspiracy theories, many of the reported incidents can be explained by natural causes such as navigational errors, severe weather, mechanical failures, and human factors (as per scientists not me). The region is heavily traveled, and incidents of disappearance are relatively rare compared to the vast number of safe crossings and flights.

The thing is what we cannot explain with known science we deny it as a hoax or something that lacks credible evidence or require a repeated happening to accept it. Since these happenings take some time to reoccur, we simply deny they exist. You have to read my book on the connection between the aliens, gods and human beings to understand if the aliens are indeed gods or if they are real and more.

The Western civilization is the newest civilization, and was founded much after the Chinese (oldest), Egyptian (second oldest), Muslim (third oldest) and Indian (Fourth oldest) civilization. The Muslims took over the oldest Egyptian civilization as they took over several parts of the world and before that the Egyptians worshiped the Sun God similar to what we see the Persians doing it. The Western civilization jump took over after the Romans adopted Christianity and the Mayan and Inca civilization existed at the same time as the Indian civilization but was destroyed during the conquest of North America by the Spaniards and others from Europe.

Traces of trade between the older civilizations do exist in some texts and found artifacts. How the languages of different civilizations differ is also a mystery and I have tried hard to understand the common thing in all of them and failed. The same things and thoughts can be spoken by different people is like one vehicle running on petrol, another on diesel and some other on gas but all of them can be cars, like all people speaking different languages are humans. If we were to remove the languages to common all humans would appear same irrespective of religion.

These things science cannot explain and they cannot deny it either and call it unexplainable because it has evidence and does not come under hoax or evolution.

If we consider Atlantis being connected with Western civilization, then the Western civilization existed much before other civilizations and is the oldest. Before the conquest by the Muslims even Egyptian and Greek civilizations can be considered as Western Civilizations for that matter and attracts the Western tourists the most.

For that matter Atlantis connection with Western civilization is as explained below:

Atlantis is a mythical island first mentioned by the ancient Greek philosopher Plato in his dialogues "Timaeus" and "Critias," written around 360 BCE. According to Plato's account, Atlantis was a powerful and advanced civilization that existed thousands of years before his time.

In Plato's dialogues, the character Critias narrates the story of Atlantis as a powerful island nation located beyond the Pillars of Hercules (usually identified as the Strait of Gibraltar). Atlantis was said to be a prosperous and advanced civilization, with impressive engineering feats and a utopian society. However, it grew corrupt and aggressive, leading to its eventual destruction by natural disasters, sinking into the ocean in a single day and night.

The tale of Atlantis has captured the imagination of scholars, historians, and enthusiasts for centuries. Many have attempted to find evidence of a lost civilization that could be linked to Plato's account, but no concrete archaeological or historical evidence supporting Atlantis's existence as described in the ancient texts has been found.

Over the centuries, numerous theories have proposed possible locations for Atlantis, ranging from the Mediterranean to the Atlantic Ocean and beyond. Some have suggested that it might have been situated in the Aegean Sea, off the coast of Spain, near the Caribbean, or even on the Antarctic continent.

Beyond its literal interpretation, Atlantis holds symbolic and moral significance. Some scholars consider the story as an allegory, representing the rise and fall of civilizations, the consequences of human hubris and greed, or the pursuit of an idealized utopia.

The story of Atlantis has had a significant impact on Western literature, philosophy, and popular culture. It continues to be referenced and reinterpreted in various artistic works, including literature, films, and video games.

While many enthusiasts find the tale of Atlantis captivating, skepticism remains among historians and archaeologists due to the lack of concrete evidence supporting its existence. Some consider the story as purely fictional, a product of Plato's imagination rather than an actual historical account.

In summary, Atlantis remains one of the great mysteries of human history, with countless theories and debates surrounding its possible existence and location. Whether based on truth or fiction, the legend of Atlantis continues to spark curiosity and fascination, leaving us to ponder the mysteries of the ancient past and the enduring allure of lost civilizations.

What they say "Throughout history, various expeditions and explorations have been conducted to find evidence of Atlantis, but none have provided definitive proof of the existence of such an advanced civilization with pyramids in the Atlantic."

Plato was a Greek and so there is relation of Greece with the Western Civilization and it may also have a link with Atlantis.

But the lack of tangible evidence of Atlantis has led many scholars, historians, and archaeologists to consider the tale as a work of fiction or an allegory by Plato rather than a real historical account. As a result, no ruins or physical remnants of Atlantis have been discovered.

Numerous theories and speculative claims have been proposed over the centuries, suggesting possible locations for Atlantis, including areas in the Mediterranean, Atlantic Ocean, Caribbean, and beyond. However, none of these theories have been supported by concrete evidence.

The search for Atlantis and any potential leftover ruins has not yielded definitive results, and it remains a subject of fascination and debate among enthusiasts and researchers.

Plato was a Greek philosopher, widely regarded as one of the most influential figures in the history of Western philosophy. He was born around 428 or 427 BCE in Athens, Greece, and he lived during the Classical period of ancient Greece.

Plato was a student of Socrates, another prominent Greek philosopher, and he went on to establish his own philosophical school known as the Academy. The Academy was a center of learning and philosophical inquiry where Plato and his followers engaged in discussions and explored various philosophical concepts.

Plato's works have had a profound impact on philosophy, mathematics, science, and various other fields. He is best known for his dialogues, where he used conversations between characters to explore philosophical ideas, ethical principles, and political theories. Some of his most famous works include "The Republic," "Symposium," "Phaedo," and "Timaeus."

Plato's philosophy covered a wide range of topics, including metaphysics, epistemology, ethics, politics, and aesthetics. He sought to understand the nature of reality, the essence of knowledge, the idea of justice, and the structure of an ideal society.

His intellectual legacy continues to influence modern philosophy and remains a fundamental part of the philosophical curriculum in universities and academic institutions around the world.

Surprisingly, all or most of the laws of the modern world have been made using philosophy and the writings and teachings of philosophers. You will have to go into detail into law and origin of governments to know that. I know it as all of it is in my mind only writing everything in books is difficult for me.

Some real happenings in Bermuda Triangle are:

Flight 19 (1945)

The disappearance of Flight 19, a group of five U.S. Navy TBM Avenger torpedo bombers, on December 5, 1945. The squadron was on a routine training mission from Fort Lauderdale, Florida, when they vanished without a trace. A rescue aircraft sent to search for them, known as "Flight 19's Mariner," also disappeared. The cause of this incident remains uncertain, but it is widely believed to be due to navigational errors and adverse weather conditions.

USS Cyclops (1918)

The USS Cyclops, a United States Navy cargo ship, went missing in the Bermuda Triangle in March 1918. The ship was carrying a large cargo of manganese ore and had a crew of over 300 people. No distress signals were sent, and no wreckage or survivors were ever found. The exact cause of the disappearance remains unknown, with theories ranging from storms to structural failures.

SS Cotopaxi (1925)

The SS Cotopaxi, a cargo ship, went missing in December 1925 while en route from Charleston, South Carolina, to Havana, Cuba. Despite extensive searches, no wreckage or survivors were found.

Star Tiger (1948)

On January 30, 1948, a British South American Airways Avro Tudor aircraft named Star Tiger disappeared while flying from Santa Maria, Azores, to Bermuda. The aircraft was carrying 25 passengers and six crew members. No trace of the aircraft or its occupants was ever found. The aircraft were traveling from Bermuda to Jamaica and then to Trinidad and disappeared with no distress signals. Despite extensive searches, no wreckage or survivors were found. The incidents remain unsolved, but it is suspected that weather and communication issues may have contributed to the disappearances.

DC-3 (1948)

I n December 1948, a Douglas DC-3 aircraft disappeared
while flying from San Juan, Puerto Rico, to Miami, Florida.
The aircraft was carrying 32 people, and no trace of it was
found.

Star Ariel (1949)

On January 17, 1949, a British South American Airways Avro Tudor aircraft named Star Ariel disappeared while flying from Bermuda to Kingston, Jamaica. The aircraft was carrying 13 passengers and seven crew members. Like Star Tiger, no wreckage or survivors were ever located.

Martin Mariner (1954)

On December 28, 1954, a United States Navy Martin P5M Mariner flying boat disappeared while on a rescue mission for a missing merchant ship in the Bermuda Triangle. The aircraft and all 10 crew members vanished without a trace.

Witchcraft (1967)

The yacht "Witchcraft" disappeared off the coast of Miami, Florida, on December 22, 1967. The yacht was known for its stability and was believed to be unsinkable. Despite extensive search efforts, no wreckage or signs of the yacht and its two occupants were found.

SS Marine Sulphur Queen (1963)

The SS Marine Sulphur Queen, a T2 tanker converted to carry molten sulfur, disappeared in February 1963 with a crew of 39 while traveling from Texas to Virginia. The ship was not carrying a distress signal when it vanished, and despite extensive search efforts, no wreckage or survivors were found. The exact cause of the disappearance remains a mystery.

Trislander Incident (2008)

In August 2008, a British International Airlines Trislander aircraft disappeared while flying over the Bermuda Triangle. The wreckage of the aircraft was found in the ocean, and all seven people on board were presumed to have died. The investigation revealed that the aircraft's right-wing engine was inoperative, which could have contributed to the incident.

While these places may be mysteries for the world, there are people living in and around Mount Kailas and the Bermuda Triangle and of course they do see some of the aerial phenomena of the lights and spacecrafts in a period of a few months. But they consider it as normal and hardly collect the required evidence. As with all local places which are ghost like, they stay away from those zones like we stay away from haunted nearby place or surroundings.

For those in contact with the Devil, since the Bermuda Triangle is often called the Devil's triangle, they feel the energy and the ones who are possessed even climb walls and stick to ceilings. This has been actually recorded by some people when someone in their house is possessed by evil spirits. From where this energy which defies comes from no one knowns. Some people visit such mysterious places or holy places to get rid of these evil spirits and energies. In other ways, the evil spirits residing within the body may detach themselves and settle in those mysterious places which offer them calm and peace. That is why in some cases people feel at eternal peace when visiting and coming back from those mysteries and holy places as if they got rid of something unwanted in their bodies.

Visits to temples, old monuments, Mount Kailas, Bermuda Triangle and some more mysterious mountains around the entire Earth is related to feel and experience this energy. Not all this energy is bad and we have even good energy which is also found in temples and some holy places and not in all religious locations depending on the pollution level.

The concept of evil spirits or negative energy is prevalent in various cultures and belief systems worldwide. It refers to malevolent supernatural entities or forces believed to cause harm, misfortune, illness, or disturbances in the physical or spiritual realms. The interpretations of evil spirits and negative energy vary significantly depending on religious, spiritual, or cultural beliefs. Here are some common perspectives on evil spirits and negative energy:

Religious Beliefs: In many religious traditions, evil spirits are considered malevolent beings or fallen angels that oppose the divine or benevolent forces. For example, in Christianity, evil spirits are often associated with demons, who are believed to be adversaries of God and humanity. Similar concepts exist in other faiths, such as Islam, Judaism, Hinduism, and various indigenous belief systems.

In spiritual practices and folklore, evil spirits may be seen as energies or entities that attach themselves to individuals or places and bring negative influences. Spiritual healers and practitioners of energy work may focus on cleansing or removing these negative energies to restore balance and harmony.

In some cultures, beliefs in evil spirits and negative energy are intertwined with superstitions. People may perform rituals or use charms and amulets to protect themselves from evil influences or bad luck.

Evil spirits often feature prominently in folklore and myths, where they may take various forms and have specific attributes. These stories often serve as cautionary tales or explanations for natural phenomena or unfortunate events.

Some psychologists interpret beliefs in evil spirits and negative energy as a manifestation of the human psyche. These beliefs may be rooted in the human need to explain and understand the complexities of life and the presence of good and evil in the world.

In the field of paranormal investigations, some individuals claim to encounter or communicate with evil spirits or negative energies during investigations of haunted locations or supernatural phenomena.

It's important to note that beliefs in evil spirits and negative energy are subjective and not universally accepted or supported by empirical evidence. What one culture or individual perceives as evil spirits or negative energy may be interpreted differently by others as positive. Cultural context, personal experiences, and individual belief systems all play a role in shaping these perspectives.

All visits to mysterious places are related to experience the good and bad energies otherwise why would people endure hardships to get there. In the night in those mysterious places there is abundance of bad energy and evil spirits as it is pitching dark thick jungle or remote place. In the morning those places are heaven, full of beauty, scenery, greenery or snow and glaciers. Both things get experienced at the same time only because those places are having less humans than in the rest of the places of the world. As humans increase in population in any place the spiritual energy diminishes.

Our minds are programmed two times in a day one in the early morning and one during sleep. It is difficult to observe this programming and who are the angels or spirits who do them.

The concepts of evil spirits energy and good spirits energy are related to the belief in supernatural forces or entities that are perceived to have positive or negative influences on individuals and their surroundings. These beliefs are prevalent in various cultural, religious, and spiritual traditions. Let's explore each concept in more detail:

Evil spirits energy refers to malevolent or negative forces, often believed to be malevolent supernatural entities or malevolent energies that can cause harm, misfortune, illness, or disturbances in the physical or spiritual realms. In some belief systems, evil spirits are seen as malevolent beings that seek to harm or create chaos in the lives of individuals or communities. They are often associated with malevolence, deception, and a desire to cause suffering.

People may hold beliefs in evil spirits energy as a way to explain unfortunate events, illnesses, or negative experiences that they cannot easily comprehend or explain.

Good spirits energy refers to benevolent or positive forces, often believed to be benevolent supernatural entities or positive energies that bring blessings, protection, healing, or positive influence.

In various belief systems, good spirits are seen as benevolent beings that guide, protect, and offer assistance to individuals or communities. They are often associated with kindness, wisdom, and a desire to bring positive outcomes.

People may hold beliefs in good spirits energy as a source of comfort, hope, and support during difficult times or as a way to express gratitude for positive experiences and blessings. These concepts of spirits energy can be found in various cultural and religious contexts, such as animistic traditions, indigenous beliefs, shamanic practices, and spiritual and metaphysical beliefs. It's important to recognize that beliefs in spirits energy, whether evil or good, are subjective and may vary significantly from one culture or individual to another.

From a scientific perspective, these beliefs fall under the category of metaphysical or supernatural beliefs and are not based on empirical evidence. As such, attitudes toward spirits energy can range from firm convictions to complete skepticism, depending on cultural, religious, and personal beliefs. Ultimately, beliefs in spirits energy play a significant role in shaping the spiritual and cultural practices of different societies and individuals, influencing rituals, ceremonies, healing practices, and interactions with the unseen or spiritual realms.

Early medicine practice used removal of spirits and evil energies to heal people and some associated illness and diseases with possession by evil spirits. Many people even get cured by such methods which have no medical facilities although not all diseases can be cured by exorcism. The Church has recognized exorcism but the practice is between uneducated people performing them in villages and ones who are educated doing them to remove evil spirits or diseases.

Mysterious mountains are natural features that have captivated human imagination and inspired various myths, legends, and mysteries throughout history. These mountains often have unique geological formations, unusual geographical features, or associations with mystical or supernatural elements. Other examples of mysterious mountains from different parts of the world also exist:

Machu Picchu (Peru)

Machu Picchu is an ancient Inca citadel situated high in the Andes Mountains of Peru. Its precise purpose and the circumstances of its abandonment by the Inca civilization remain a mystery. The city's dramatic location and its engineering marvels continue to fascinate archaeologists and tourists alike.

Mount Shasta (California, USA)

Mount Shasta is a dormant volcano located in California, known for its large size and distinct conical shape. It is a significant site in Native American mythology and has been associated with various supernatural and extraterrestrial claims, making it a center of interest for UFO enthusiasts and spiritual seekers.

Mount Everest (Nepal and China)

Mount Everest, the world's tallest mountain, has long held a mystique and allure for adventurers and mountaineers. It remains a challenging and dangerous destination for climbers, and numerous stories of heroic feats and tragedies have contributed to its legendary status.

Mount Fuji (Japan)

Mount Fuji is an iconic and active volcano in Japan, considered a symbol of the country's cultural and spiritual heritage. Its near-perfect cone shape and the association with Shinto and Buddhist beliefs have made it a subject of reverence and inspiration in Japanese art and literature.

Mount Ararat (Turkey)

Mount Ararat is believed to be the resting place of Noah's Ark, as mentioned in the biblical account of the Great Flood. Numerous expeditions have sought to find evidence of the Ark's existence on the mountain, contributing to its enduring mystery.

Mount Roraima (Venezuela, Guyana, Brazil)

Mount Roraima is a tabletop mountain located in the border region of Venezuela, Guyana, and Brazil. Its unique flat-topped appearance and its association with the mystical "Lost World" inspired Sir Arthur Conan Doyle's novel "The Lost World."

These mysterious mountains continue to evoke wonder, curiosity, and intrigue, attracting tourists, adventurers, and those seeking a connection with the unknown or the spiritual. While many of the mysteries surrounding these mountains are based on folklore, mythology, and cultural beliefs, they contribute to the timeless appeal of these majestic natural landmarks.

There are several mysterious places around the world, similar to the Bermuda Triangle, where unexplained events, disappearances, or unusual phenomena have been reported. These places have sparked fascination and speculation for decades, often leading to various theories and legends. Here are some mysterious locations that share similarities with the Bermuda Triangle:

The Devil's Sea (Japan)

Also known as the Dragon's Triangle, this area in the Pacific Ocean off the coast of Japan is often considered the Asian counterpart to the Bermuda Triangle. It has a reputation for numerous ship and aircraft disappearances, as well as reports of electronic malfunctions and unusual weather patterns.

Lake Michigan Triangle (USA)

S ituated in the Great Lakes region of the United States, the Lake Michigan Triangle is known for mysterious shipwrecks and aircraft disappearances. Some accounts suggest similar phenomena to the Bermuda Triangle, including sudden storms and unexplained navigational errors.

Bennington Triangle (Vermont, USA)

This region in southwestern Vermont gained attention due to a series of mysterious disappearances in the mid-20th century. People and even entire groups reportedly vanished without a trace, leading to legends of paranormal activity and unexplained phenomena.

Hoia Baciu Forest (Romania)

Often referred to as the "Bermuda Triangle of Transylvania," this forest is located near Cluj-Napoca, Romania. It is known for numerous reports of strange occurrences, including UFO sightings, unexplained lights, and accounts of people getting lost and experiencing unexplained physical symptoms.

The Bridgewater Triangle (Massachusetts, USA)

This area in southeastern Massachusetts is infamous for reports of paranormal and unexplained phenomena. It encompasses numerous reports of UFO sightings, ghostly encounters, and mysterious animal mutilations.

The Alaska Triangle (USA)

This vast wilderness in Alaska is associated with unexplained aircraft disappearances and mysteries. The area includes the Alaska Range, the Barren Islands, and the Copper River Delta.

The South Atlantic Anomaly

Although not a specific location like the Bermuda Triangle, this is an area in the South Atlantic Ocean where the Earth's magnetic field is unusually weak. It has been associated with anomalies in satellite communication and has sparked speculation about potential effects on electronic systems.

It's essential to approach these mysterious places with critical thinking and recognize that many reports and legends may have natural or conventional explanations. Some locations may have gained a reputation for unexplained events due to a combination of human imagination, folklore, and selective reporting of incidents. Nonetheless, these enigmatic places continue to captivate the human imagination and remain subjects of fascination and exploration.

There is no scientific evidence to support the existence of any paranormal or mysterious phenomena in the area or it has not been researched.

Bruce Gernon (1970)

Bruce Gernon, a pilot and businessman, reported a mysterious and rapid time-travel-like experience while flying through the Bermuda Triangle in 1970. He claimed that his aircraft encountered a strange cloud tunnel that seemed to warp time, shortening his flight duration significantly compared to standard travel times. He coined this phenomenon the "Electronic Fog."

Ellen Austin (1881)

The Ellen Austin, a schooner, reportedly came across an abandoned and mysterious ghost ship in the Bermuda Triangle in 1881. The crew of the Ellen Austin boarded the derelict vessel to find no signs of the crew, but they decided to tow it back to port. However, a storm separated the two ships, and the derelict ship vanished again, leaving the crew of the Ellen Austin baffled.

Mount Kailash has been associated with some UFO (Unidentified Flying Object) sightings and claims of extraterrestrial activity. UFO sightings and related claims are often subject to various interpretations, and many can be attributed to natural phenomena, misidentifications, hoaxes, or simply a lack of understanding about the observed events.

Regarding Mount Kailash, some UFO enthusiasts and conspiracy theorists have suggested that the mountain's remote location and its spiritual significance may attract extraterrestrial beings or unidentified aerial phenomena. Which means like we visit tourist places the aliens may also be visiting some attractions of the Earth or military aircrafts may be trying to explore these places as entry of military and government aircrafts are banned to those location in view of sensitivity of religion beliefs.

Till such time religious beliefs exist the military and other governments stay clear of holy and ancient sites and they themselves are afraid of severe consequences in case the mystery box is opened and nothing is found. Spirits don't have traces and cannot leave evidences, that fact is not understood by the scientific and research community.

Government finances such research through grants and other help but generally do not directly participate in such missions of research as even their missions have ended in disasters and the mission crew getting killed or disappearing in un natural circumstances including storms and the like.

While some governments may not dedicate significant resources to investigating mysterious places, there are private and academic organizations and individuals with a keen interest in exploring such phenomena. These groups often conduct independent research, but their findings may not always be widely accepted by the scientific community. Scientific exploration and curiosity about the unknown continue to be pursued by individuals and organizations around the world, contributing to ongoing discoveries and knowledge in various fields.

It's essential to recognize that the term "mysterious places" encompasses a wide range of phenomena, from natural wonders with scientific explanations to claims of the paranormal, supernatural, or extraterrestrial. Government actions and decisions related to research are often shaped by a complex interplay of scientific, social, political, and cultural factors.

The claim that governments are afraid to research mysterious places is not universally applicable and may not accurately reflect the actions or attitudes of all governments worldwide

Governments allocate their resources based on priorities that align with national interests, security, and the well-being of their citizens. Researching mysterious places may not always be seen as a priority compared to other pressing issues, such as healthcare, infrastructure, or national security. Mysterious places are often associated with unexplained phenomena or paranormal claims. From a scientific perspective, extraordinary claims require extraordinary evidence. Governments may be hesitant to invest resources in researching phenomena that lack credible scientific evidence or are widely regarded as pseudoscience.

Governments are accountable to their citizens, and investing taxpayer money in researching mysterious places without clear scientific objectives may be seen as a misuse of public funds. Public perception and concerns about government credibility can influence decisions about research priorities.

In some cases, mysterious places may intersect with sensitive military or national security areas. Governments might be reluctant to disclose certain information to the public, leading to perceptions of secrecy or fear. Governments might be cautious about researching mysterious places, particularly if it involves crossing international borders or interfering with other countries' territories. Such actions could potentially strain diplomatic relations.

Some mysterious places might have cultural or religious significance to local populations. Governments may exercise caution to respect the beliefs and traditions of indigenous communities and avoid disrupting their sacred sites.

The scientific community may not uniformly agree on the validity or importance of researching mysterious places. This lack of consensus can impact government decision-making on research priorities. It's essential to recognize that the term "mysterious places" encompasses a wide range of phenomena, from natural wonders with scientific explanations to claims of the paranormal, supernatural, or extraterrestrial. Government actions and decisions related to research are often shaped by a complex interplay of scientific, social, political, and cultural factors.

While we are sending space missions to the moon, Mars and beyond, someday even those missions will be banned and stopped and like religious and mysterious places became not allowed in future when we suffer similar supernatural happenings as we see on Mount Kailas, other mountains, Bermuda Triangle and other places on Earth. Then Space may not seem as rosy and adventurous as it is seen today.

We may have Bermuda Triangle like situations while travelling to Mars or maybe the Moon. Nothing can be confirmed unless we have a lot of successful missions.

The Apollo program included a total of 17 missions, with six of them successfully landing astronauts on the lunar surface. The most well-known and significant of these missions was Apollo 11, which successfully landed the first humans on the Moon on July 20, 1969, with Neil Armstrong and Buzz Aldrin taking those historic steps.

After the success of Apollo 11, several more missions followed, each building upon the knowledge and experience gained from previous flights. These missions included scientific research, exploring different regions of the Moon, and conducting experiments.

The Apollo program eventually came to an end due to a combination of factors:

The Apollo program was expensive, and the U.S. government faced increasing pressure to allocate funds to other national priorities, including social programs and the Vietnam War. After the initial excitement of landing on the Moon, public interest and support for further lunar missions declined. The program faced diminishing public enthusiasm, which influenced government decisions.

By the early 1970s, NASA had achieved the primary scientific objective of demonstrating the capability to land on the Moon and return safely. The agency had also gathered valuable data and samples from the lunar surface. As the space program evolved, NASA shifted its focus to other projects, such as the Skylab space station and later, the Space Shuttle program.

While the Apollo program was a remarkable achievement, it faced technological limitations in terms of sustainable lunar exploration. Long-term colonization of the Moon would require substantial resources and infrastructure beyond the program's capabilities. Even today a Moon mission requires 100 billion dollars for one visit and maybe the Mars mission may cost 500 billion dollars. That is a huge amount of money and all of it can come only from taxes. That is how ancient civilizations became bankrupt spending on wars, technology and exploration. There is no limit to exploration and for governments exploration by individuals is much cheaper and less risky loss of manpower.

Even governments know these mysteries exist and places which are haunted even the 911 emergency services keep of it.

The last crewed mission of the Apollo program was Apollo 17, which landed on the Moon in December 1972. After that, the Apollo program was officially ended. Now after several decades we are trying to go to the Moon as if it is new Technology and we are not even having that old Technology which took us to the Moon in the first place and neither are we able to replicate it.

Efforts to return humans to the Moon have been revisited in recent years, with initiatives such as NASA's Artemis program aiming to establish sustainable lunar exploration and prepare for future missions to Mars.

One day all of this will link in the future as our science advances to a level where we can understand these things or we perish before it like the great floods where everything went down under water to be regenerated again before and after Atlantis and the Noah's ark. There have been no widely accepted archaeological finds definitively confirming the existence of the legendary city of Atlantis as per historians or scientific community. Without definitive evidence or corroborating historical sources, Atlantis remains a tantalizing mystery and a subject of fascination in popular culture, literature, and speculative discussions.

Some stories claim that pilots and sailors traveling through the Bermuda Triangle have experienced time warps or encountered strange "electronic fog" that caused navigational equipment to malfunction and disoriented them.

The aliens or the people living in underground civilizations have powers that can jam electronic machinery. I don't know if this is known to the world. The flying saucers are also believed to belong to them and they also have supernatural powers. Some day or later when the population of humans grows beyond manageable size, they will encounter these alien beings living in underground civilizations and there may be a war the result of which may be similar to what happened on Mars.

At least people don't travel underground beyond a certain point and some civilizations such as the Chinese, Buddhist and Hindu civilizations do mention the underground world. But for the Hindus the underground world is full of snake people and Lord Shiva and Lord Krishna their gods have link with snakes. Lord Shiva always has a snake around his neck and Lord Krishna sleeps and rests on snakes.

It is also told in ancient Hindu history and in some other mythological texts of snakes having ability to become humans and vice versa and some Gods belonging to the serpentine meaning they come from the snakes or are part of the snake dynasty. In fact, some Gods of other religions also have relation to snakes or having snakes wrapped around some part of their body or at the back near the spinal cord. Not to be afraid the spinal cord is associated with shape of a snake and most of all living beings have a spinal cord. But it is a fiction of imagination rather than reality.

All of us have snake dreams in some part of our life and we always wonder how do the shapes are prestored in our mind and why they haunt us and then go away. Some mysteries are endless and impossible beyond research and even imagination.

Lord Shiva and Lord Krishna (also known as Rama, Ram, Vishnu) always connected themselves with the snake king living underground when on Earth in their avatars or something when they take birth in human form.

Some Gods can even enter our bodies and make us feel as if we are gods and I saw this problem for many years with one of the Hindu gods occupying my body. I therefore though that all of the knowledge I have or had in this life is due to them entering my body. I was very difficult to get rid of them and even today it is difficult although I have recovered more than 80 % though self-will and determinedness.

I believe in Gods but if gods are capable, they are having the required spiritual energy to become humans and should not require to possess other human bodies. One God I know who is similar to Lord Krishna or Vishnu claims to be commander of the Galatic forces controlling several planets and solar systems. He can be born at several places all at the same time and be at several places at the same time. This is to show you how much I know about them but they are clever and avoid direct contact.

I become afraid standing even one second in space and therefore it becomes difficult to explore space and time and other planets as much as I want. The fear of losing my body on Earth with people thinking me dead results in me coming back to my body instantly.

Gods don't like people with more knowledge than what is required and several people possessing superficial knowledge are desisted not only by society but also by gods and often see premature death.

The Galactic force is said to have thousands of spaceships, huge super computers and flying saucers. It took control of our solar system around 5000 years back and may have been responsible in destroying Atlantis and Mars. Their faces are non-human like and are humanoids unlike the gods who look like humans. The Galactic force is more powerful than our gods but they have no spiritual powers like our gods. They are machine based like the machines we have. That is one of the reasons that all magical powers have disappeared from Earth and now we run only on machines.

While the Galactic force claims Lord Krishna is their commander, that thing is not possible as the people of Galactic force have weak bodies like the ones, we see of aliens on Earth but they have more of machine power enough to destroy any planet fully like Mars. It is impossible for someone like me to fight the powerful Galactic forces. We are watching them and they are watching us that is the only thing that is going on since maybe last 2000 years or so after destruction of Mars.

Did you love *Secrets of Mount Kailash, Bermuda Triangle and the Lost City of Atlantis*? Then you should read *The Maid & The Mansion's Secret*[1] by Jagdish Arora!

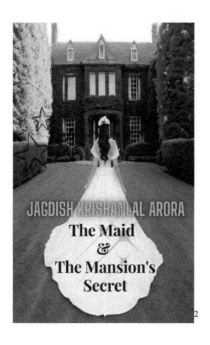

"The Maid and the Mansion's Secret" invites readers into a world of intrigue and hidden truths. As Maria the Housemaid navigates her role within the opulent estate, she becomes entangled in a web of deception, unearthing mysteries that challenge privilege and vulnerability. This captivating tale explores the resilience of the human spirit, the pursuit of truth, and the unexpected connections that can shape destinies. Join us on a journey where uncovering secrets comes at a cost, but

1. https://books2read.com/u/bPeD6A

2. https://books2read.com/u/bPeD6A

the rewards are immeasurable. Embark on a narrative that lingers beyond the final page, reminding us that even within the confines of a mansion, courage can rewrite history.

Also by Jagdish Arora

A NEW BEGINNING
The Struggling Author
The Bhagavad Gita English Version
A Werewolf's Tale of Love and Destiny
Basic Inorganic and Organic Chemistry
Book of Jokes
Car Insurance and Claims
DIGITAL ELECTRONICS, COMPUTER
ARCHITECTURE AND MICROPROCESSOR DESIGN
PRINCIPLES
Guided Meditation and Yoga
Master the ACT: 2023-2024 Exam Preparation Guide
The Bible and Jesus Christ
The Lost Son
The Maid & The Mansion's Secret
Unity Quest
Secrets of Mount Kailash, Bermuda Triangle and the Lost
City of Atlantis

Milton Keynes UK
Ingram Content Group UK Ltd.
UKHW010653250923
429338UK00001B/11